Practice What Yuh Preach

How Fi Grow Yuh Pickney Book 3

Written By Catherine Alexander-McDaniel

Illustrated By Krystal Ball

Contributions By Zunammie Keren

Joshua and Jacob

- My love for you is what keeps me going. I want nothing more than for you both to grow up with values and be valued. I'm proud to be your Mom.

A Note to Parents/Guardians/Teachers

This series is a plea for us all to do our part in ensuring that we are good examples for children to follow.

As a mother of 2 boys, I was inspired to write these books as I noticed that more and more children lack basic manners and respect. It is my view that our 'village' is failing us. Because of our busy lives, we depend on schools to protect and teach them what should be reinforced and practised in the home. We don't spend the time monitoring what our children are exposed to from the TV, social media and the Internet. We need to sit and explain our religious beliefs and core values and pray for them daily.

These books are for us just as much as they are for the children. Please read together to spark a discussion on core values. Let us also examine ourselves. 'Do as I say and not as I do' cannot be the answer.

We cannot continue to allow our values and morals to be depleted which steer our children to add to the breakdown of our beautiful country, Jamaica.

Let us fight for our children. They are worth it, are they not?

Practice What Yuh Preach

It was a hot day and a long walk to the patty shop. For the first time, Jacob was allowed to walk with his older brother to the store to get patties for lunch.

'Jeeezam, look how di line long!' his older brother Joshua exclaimed as they pushed open the door.

Jacob, even though hot and hungry, was happy to be there regardless of the line. He looked around and decided quickly that he wanted a chicken patty. And a Pepsi too!

An older gentleman stepped in front of him and bounced his shoulder as he passed.

'Join the line nuh Jacob, before everybody skip yuh. I need to go ova di side to get the phone credit fah Daddy' his brother instructed.

Jacob didn't mind the wait. He liked the excitement of the busy shop and took in what was going on around him. Because he was the youngest in the family, he often had to stay at home with his auntie while everyone else got to do as they liked.

While waiting in the line, Jacob first noticed the cashier. She didn't smile or greet any of the customers. As a matter of fact she never said a word and her facial expression only changed when a man insisted she shorted him $100 (after which he found it) and she cut her eye after him.

He noticed customers taking their food from the servers without a thank you. He saw two men tease an overweight boy in the line about how many patties it would take to fill his belly. He even saw a very uppity-looking woman step quickly ahead of an old lady in line while she wasn't looking.

Jacob was a little confused about what was happening around him. This wasn't at all how his family acted. He was always told to be polite, have manners and be respectful. Maybe all these people were just joking around?

His thoughts were interrupted by a man bawling out loudly way at the back of the line.

'Princess! How yuh move suh slow! Cash di people dem fassa before mi get angry inna di shop! Mi hungry y'nuh!' as he kissed his teeth and continued mumbling to himself and all who would listen.

As Jacob approached the front of the line he was quite amused by all the people in the shop joking around. He decided he was going to joke around too! He laughed to himself as he rehearsed what he was going to say to the cashier.

He felt the cashier's eyes on him as he stepped up to the counter. 'Yow Princess, gimme 6 patty an 4 Pepsi, yuh sime?'

All of a sudden the patty shop went quiet. The cashier who hadn't said a word to anyone opened her eyes wide.

'Wha yuh jus seh to mi likkle pickney?' she replied angrily.

Joshua came running up when he heard the commotion to see his little brother in a state of fright.

'No, no Miss....sorry Miss.... I...I was just running a joke like the man at the back of the line!' Jacob stuttered.

'Leave him alone' a voice said from the line.

It was the old lady.

'Listen to yourselves!' she began. 'Pay attention to your own actions. This child is learning from all of us! He's so confused by what he's hearing and seeing that he thinks you are all joking!'

She continued 'You over there with your bad language!' she pointed to the man who was shouting at the cashier. 'You must do better than that and be a good example for children to follow!'

The man nodded and kept quiet.

'You Miss who never smile in the 5 years I've been coming here' she pointed to the cashier. 'A simple smile or a kind greeting can set the tone for someone's day!

The cashier hung down her head.

'And all of you need to learn to say thank you when the servers give you your order. Its a way of showing respect and having manners!'

The servers smiled and cheered.

'And finally, You Miss Uptown Lady! You think I didn't see when you stepped ahead of me in the line?'

The lady nearly choked on her patty.

The old lady patted Jacob.

'Son, you should always speak to people with respect. Give respect and you get back respect. That is a lesson for everyone in here.'

The loud man at the back of the line replied first 'Sometimes mi nuh really watch what mi sayin and mi ave a likkle yout like yuh. Mi really sorry mi bawl out like that and disrespek di people dem. Mi should jus wait mi turn and calm dung'.

'Is true Ma'am' the cashier replied. 'My granny always told me that it tek a village to raise a child and all a we is part a di village. I gwine do betta, yuh ere dahlin'?' as she practised her smile.

'We were not very good examples for him to follow. I apologize also' said Ms Uppity Lady.

Joshua took his little brothers hand and said 'Jacob, beg yuh use yuh mannas and ask fi di patty dem please? Mi hungry bad now!'

All the people in the shop clapped and cheered as Jacob asked for his food politely and was served with a smile.

The End

Mannas tek yuh thru di worl

(Having good manners is the key to getting you through life)

Thank You for reading!

How Fi Grow Yuh Pickney Book 3
Practice What Yuh Preach

The Author

Catherine was born in Montreal and raised in Jamaica since age 7. She is a sales professional and the mother of 2 boys - Joshua 11 and Jacob 7. This is her first book series intended to revive values and bring more awareness to our own actions.

The Illustrator

Krystal Ball is a Jamaican artist who officially entered the international art scene after winning the Pan American Health Organization's Centennial Poster Competition at the tender age of 10 years old. She has continued to practice art throughout her life after returning from her studies in Philadelphia to reside in Jamaica where she is currently studying Chemistry and is an art instructor.

The Contributor

Zunammie Keren is a Jamaican freelancer writer. She writes books, articles and other web content. Zunammie enjoys reading, writing and spending time at the beach with her husband and their 3 sons.

How Fi Grow Yuh Pickney Series